INDIAN · CUISINE
Balti

INDIAN * CUISINE

* Balti *

Tiger Books International

London

Acknowledgement:
Grateful thanks to Madhu Arora, Kiran Kapoor and Mili Paul
for having tried, tested and making available
the dishes for photography.

This edition published in 1996 by:
Tiger Books International PLC, Twickenham

ISBN: 1-85501-812-8

Project Coordinator:
Arti Arora

Production:
N.K. Nigam, Gautam Dey, Abhijeet Raha

Conceived & Designed by:
Pramod Kapoor
at
Roli Books CAD Centre

Photographer:
Dheeraj Paul

Other photographs by:
Neeraj Paul: Cover and 2, 11, 22, 30, 48, 66

Printed and bound by:
Star Standard Industries Pte. Ltd., Singapore

CONTENTS

*

▲ *Kadhai* (Wok)

Belan (Rolling pin) ▲ - *Chakla* (Flour board)

Tawa (Griddle) ▶

Chimta (Tongs) ▶

Kaddoo kas (Grater) ▼

Masaaldaan ▶ (Spice container)

Hamam dasta (Mortar pestle) ▼

Handi (Heavy-bottomed pot) ▼

Karchi (Ladles) ▶

Pateela (Deep pot) ▼

TO GET YOU AQUAINTED.....

Balti or Stir-fry cooking derives its name from the quick and easy technique employed for the delicious preparation of Indian dishes. Spices in this style, dominate the contents, since they have a strong taste and fragrance which gives flexibility to the principal ingredient.

The main utensil used for this kind of cooking is a cast iron *kadhai*, similar to the Chinese wok. Cooking oil is heated in the *kadhai* and depending on the recipe, fresh herbs like onion, garlic and ginger or spices like *jeera* (cumin), *raee* (mustard seeds) or *kalonji* (onion seeds) are added. To this, the meats or vegetables are added for a *bhunav*, which literally is roasting. *Bhunav* is the basic cooking style for most Indian food and left at this stage, the food can be served as a dry dish or even as a snack. However, if a sauce is required, simply add water, yoghurt or coconut milk soon after the *bhunav* stage. The resultant gravy should never be watery, it must always have a consistency which also determines whether it will be eaten with rice or bread.

Indian cuisine has a range and variety that is extraordinary, with each region contributing its own flavour. Modern Indian cooking borrows selectively from these diverse styles, assimilates and adapts them to suit the palate. The richness of Indian food, therefore continues to grow.

Regional differences in food are often so great that they make for entirely different cuisines. Perhaps, what is common are the raw ingredients, the vegetables and meats, and the spices. But, while the greater part of India is vegetarian, there are other regions where meat and chicken are considered an essential part of the daily meal. In Bengal, fish is an obsession and is referred to as *jal toru*, an underwater vegetable.

Indian food is usually eaten without starters, soups or courses, though in restaurants it is presented in this manner for less familiar diners. The main meal is eaten with either rice or *roti*, and includes at least one lentil curry called *daal*, a selection of vegetarian servings, a meat, chicken or fish fry, a sampling of chutneys and pickles, and *dahi* (yoghurt). *Papads* are served with meals that may be sometimes accompanied by *lassi* (buttermilk) which helps to induce sleep on a warm afternoon! Desserts are not standard. Sweets, of course, are served with almost any Indian meal, and may take the form of a South Indian *halwa*, a delicate Lucknavi *kheer* or light Bengali sweets. But, depending on the region, these may be served after, during or before an Indian meal. No wonder Indian food continues to surprise — its serving and style almost as variable as its thousands of recipes.

Tej patta (Bay leaves)   *Methi dana* (Fenugreek seed)   *Khus khus* (Poppy seeds)   *Ajwain* (Carom seeds)   *Javitri* (Mace)

Raee (Mustard seeds)   *Haldi* (Turmeric powder)   *Choti elaichi* (Green cardamom)   *Heeng* (Asafoetida)   *Laung* (Cloves)

Bari elaichi (Black cardamom)   *Amchur* (Green mango powder)   *Laal mirch* (Red chilli)   *Dhania* (Coriander) *powder*   *Kaali mirch* (Black peppercorn)

SPICES — THE SWEET & SOUR OF INDIAN FOOD

The secret of Indian cuisine lies in its spices. Used lightly but in exciting combinations, they can leave the palate tingling for more, without actually taking a toll on one's digestion.

As the story goes, the West had discovered and traded with pockets of the Indian subcontinent, primarily for its rich spices.

Although, the beneficial uses of spices have been recorded in ancient treatises, but the usage has known to vary from region to region. Apart from making food palatable, spices also have inherent 'cooling' and 'warming' properties. They are added to the foods intended for pregnant women, for invalids, for the old and of course for the very young, to aid recovery or to impart stamina.

The basic Indian spices alongwith salt, are *jeera* (**cumin**) to impart fragrance to food, *haldi* (*turmeric*) to give colour and *laal mirch* (**red chilli**) to spice up the food. *Amchur* (*dry mango powder*) adds piquancy and a mere pinch of *heeng* (**asafoetida**) adds a unique taste and also aids digestion. Fresh **coriander** is the most common garnish and also adds a light fragrance.

Since fruits are seen as energy-giving, **dried fruits** are used extensively in India. Parts of fruits, berries or vegetables are dried and stored, as condiments. Several seeds too are used, each with a marked taste.

Saunf (**fennel**) is added to desserts and some vegetarian dishes to act as a flavouring agent. *Methi dana* (**fenugreek seeds**) gives a touch of bitterness, *kalonji* (**onion seeds**) is used in 'heavier' cooking or for pickles. *Raee* (**mustard seeds**) adds sourness to food while *khus-khus* (**poppy seeds**) enhances the flavour of meat. Fresh *imli* (**tamarind**) imparts a sour taste and *kesar* (**saffron**), India's most expensive herb, imparts a fine fragrance alongwith a rich yellow colour.

That Indian spices can be used almost in any fashion and to enhance any taste, is obvious from the fact that Indian tea too uses spices!! *Elaichi* (**cardamom**) is added to tea for flavouring, while saffron and almonds are added to *kahwa* (Kashmiri tea).

BASIC INDIAN RECIPES

Coconut chutney: Grated **coconut** (160 gms), roasted **gram** (15 gms), **curry leaves** (8), **green chillies,** chopped (5), **ginger,** chopped (15 gms), **lentils (*urad daal*),** (5 gms), **mustard seeds** (5 gms), **oil** (15 ml) and **salt** (to taste). Grind coconut, green chillies, ginger and gram to a paste. Sauté mustard seeds, lentils and curry leaves. Stir in the ground paste, cook for 3-5 minutes. Allow to cool, refrigerate and use when required.

Garam masala (for 445 gms): Finely grind the following ingredients and store: **cumin seeds** (90 gms), **black pepper corns** (70 gms), **black cardamom seeds** (75 gms), **fennel seeds** (30 gms), **green cardamoms** (40 gms), **coriander seeds** (30 gms), **cloves** (20 gms), **cinnamon sticks** (20 x 2.5 cm), **mace powder** (20 gms), **black cumin seeds** (20 gms), **dry rose petals** (15 gms), **bay leaves** (15 gms), **ginger powder** (15 gms).

Ginger paste or **Garlic paste:** Soak **ginger / garlic cloves** (300 gms) overnight to soften the skin. Peel and chop roughly. Process until pulped. The pulp can be stored in an airtight container and refrigerated for 4-6 weeks.

Green Chilli paste: Take required quantity of **green chillies**, chop roughly and process until pulped.

Khoya: Boil **milk** (2 lts) in a *kadhai* (wok). Simmer till quantity is reduced to half, stirring occasionally. Continue cooking, now stirring constantly and scraping from the sides, till a thick paste-like consistency is obtained (1-1½ hrs.). Allow to cool.

Mint Chutney: Mint leaves (60 gms), **coriander leaves** (120 gms), **cumin seeds** (5 gms), **garlic cloves** (2), **green chilli** (1), **raw mango** (30 gms), **tomatoes** (45 gms), **salt** (to taste). Chop all ingredients, blend until paste-like. Refrigerate in an airtight container.

Onion paste: Peel and chop the **onions** (500 gms) in quarters. Process until pulped. Refrigerate in an airtight container for 4-6 weeks. For **Browned Onion Paste**, slice and fry the onions in a little oil, allow to cool before processing.

Paneer (Cottage Cheese): In a pot, put **milk** (3 lts) to boil. Just before it boils, add (90 ml/6 tbs) **lemon juice / vinegar** to curdle the milk. Strain the curdled milk through a muslin cloth, to allow all whey and moisture to drain. Still wrapped in the muslin, place **paneer** under a weight for 2-3 hours to allow to set into a block which can be cut or grated.

Coconut chutney

Garam Masala

Ginger-garlic paste

Green chilli paste

Khoya

Mint Chutney

Onion paste

Paneer

CHICKEN

Exotic Chicken Dumplings (recipe on following page) ▶

Exotic Chicken Dumplings

Serves: 4   Preparation time: 25 minutes   Cooking time: 1½ hours

Ingredients:

For the dumplings:

Chicken, minced .... *1 kg*
Cumin (*jeera*) powder ....*3 gms / ½ tsp*
Black cumin (*shah jeera*)
powder .... *a pinch*
Black cardamom (*bari elaichi*)
powder ....*3 gms / ½ tsp*
Cinnamon (*daalchini*) powder ....*a pinch*
Black cardamom (*bari elaichi*) *3*
Asafoetida (*heeng*) .... *small pinch*
Red chilli powder ....*5 gms / 1 tsp*
Mustard oil ....*40 ml / 2 ⅔ tbs*
Fennel (*saunf*) seed powder......*6 gms / 1 tsp*

For the stuffing:

Dried plums (*aloo bukhara*) .... *100 gms*

For the curry:

Mustard oil ....*100 ml / ½ cup*
Cloves (*laung*) *4*
Red chilli powder ....*15 gms / 1 tbs*
Water ....*1½ ltr / 7 cups*
Green cardamoms (*choti elaichi*) *4*
Black cardamoms (*bari elaichi*) *4*
Bay leaves (*tej patta*) *2*
Black cumin (*shah jeera*) .... *2 gms / ⅓ tsp*
Salt to taste
Turmeric (*haldi*) powder ....*10 gms / 2 tsp*
Black cardamom (*bari elaichi*)
powder ....*10 gms / 2 tsp*
Fennel (*saunf*) powder ....*15 gms / 1 tbs*
Cinnamon (*daalchini*) powder *6 gms / 1 tsp*
Tomatoes, chopped ....*200 gms / 1 cup*

Method:

1. **For the dumplings**, combine all the ingredients, mix well and divide into 16 equal portions.

2. Place one dried plum in the centre of each portion. Shape into balls and keep aside.

3. **For the curry**, heat oil in *kadhai* (wok) till it is smoking. Add the cloves, when they begin to crackle, reduce the flame.

4. Add red chilli powder, wait for oil to turn red, add water and bring to a boil.

5. Mix in the remaining whole spices, powdered spices and condiments. Bring to a boil and add the chicken dumplings gently.

6. Cook for 25-30 minutes, till the curry thickens and the dumplings are fully cooked.

7. Remove into a serving dish and serve hot, accompanied by any Indian bread.

◀ *Picture on preceding page*

Chicken Raan

Serves: 4   Preparation time: 30 minutes   Cooking time: 45 minutes

Ingredients:

Chicken drumsticks .... *800 gms*
Ginger paste (page 10) ....*30 gms / 2 tbs*
Garlic paste (page 10) ....*30 gms / 2 tbs*
Salt to taste
Red chilli powder ....*5 gms / 1 tsp*
Lemon juice ....*30 ml / 2 tbs*
Brown onion paste (page 10) *90 gms / 6 tbs*
Tomato purée .... *1 lt / 4½ cups*

Chicken stock .... *1 lt / 4½ cups*
Butter (unsalted) ....*90 gms / 6 tbs*
Coriander powder ....*10 gms / 2 tsp*
Green chillies, sliced 2
Cashewnuts, roasted, crushed *15 gms / 1 tbs*
Cream ....,*30 ml / 2 tbs*
Saffron (*kesar*) dissolved in 1 tsp water ....
....*a pinch*

Method:

1. Marinate the chicken in ginger and garlic pastes, salt, chilli powder and lemon juice for an hour.

2. Skewer the drumsticks and roast in a tandoor till half done.

3. Combine the onion paste, tomato purée alongwith the chicken stock in a *kadhai* (wok). Cook on moderate heat, stirring continuously, till it reaches a sauce-like consistency. Strain the sauce through a muslin cloth and keep aside.

4. In a separate *kadhai* (wok), heat butter (4 tbs), add coriander powder and chicken drumsticks, sauté for 3-4 minutes, add the sauce and cook for another 3-4 minutes.

5. Transfer to a serving bowl and keep aside.

6. Melt the remaining butter in a small pan. Add the green chillies and sauté briefly. Add the cashewnuts and cream, pour over the prepared drumsticks. Sprinkle saffron over the cashew-cream paste.

7. Serve hot, accompanied by any Indian bread of your choice.

Stir-fried Chicken with Spring Onions

Serves: 4   Preparation time: 15 minutes   Cooking time: 1 hour

Ingredients:

Chicken, cut into boneles cubes ...... *800 gms*
Onion, chopped ....*200 gms / 1 cup*
Tomato, finely chopped .... *100 gms / ½ cup*
Mustard oil .... *80 ml / 5 ²/₃ tbs*
Mustard (*raee*) seeds .... *10 gms / 2 tsp*
Red chilli powder to taste

Salt to taste
Cumin (*jeera*) powder .... *10 gms / 2 tsp*
Ginger-Garlic paste (page 10) ....
.... *50 gms / 3 ²/₃ tbs*
Spring onion, leaves .... *100 gms / ½ cup*

Method:

1. Heat oil (2 tbs) in a *kadhai* (wok), sauté onion till transparent. Add tomatoes and cook for 10-15 minutes. Keep aside.

2. In a separate *kadhai* (wok), heat the remaining oil, add mustard seeds and sauté till they crackle.

3. Stir in the onion-tomato mixture, cook for 3-4 minutes. Add the the chicken, salt and red chilli powder.

4. Cook further for 20 minutes on low heat, till the chicken is done.

5. Mix in the spring onion, cook for 2 minutes.

6. Remove from heat and serve hot, accompanied by any Indian bread.

Chicken Almond Steaks

Serves: 4   Preparation time: 15-20 minutes   Cooking time: 30-40 minutes

Ingredients:

Chicken escalope (8 pieces) .... *600 gms*
Egg *1*
Salt .... *12 gms / 2 1/3 tsp*
White pepper powder .... *4 gms / 3/4 tsp*
Red chilli powder .... *7 gms / 1 1/3 tsp*
Lemon .... *25 gms / 5 tsp*
Ginger-Garlic paste (page 10)   *25 gms / 5 tsp*
For the sauce:
Butter, melted .... *30 gms / 2 tbs*

Almonds .... *70 gms / 4 2/3 tbs*
Oil .... *10 gms / 2 tsp*
Yoghurt .... *100 gms / 1/2 cup*
Tomato purée .... *70 gms / 4 2/3 tbs*
Brown onion paste, (page 10)   *30 gms / 2 tbs*
Cream .... *50 gms / 3 2/3 tbs*
Garam masala (page 10) .... *a pinch*

Method:

1. Make a paste of egg, salt, red chilli powder, lemon and half of the ginger-garlic paste.

2. Flatten the chicken escalopes. Coat both sides of the escalopes with butter and refrigerate for 15 minutes.

3. Blanch the almonds and grind to a paste.

4. Heat oil in a pan and shallow fry the chicken escalopes on low heat till golden brown in colour, remove and set aside.

5. **For the sauce**, mix together the almond paste and yoghurt.

6. Heat butter and oil in a frying pan.

7. Add the remaining ginger-garlic paste to the yoghurt and almond paste and sauté.

8. Season to taste with salt, red chili powder and white pepper powder.

9. Add brown onion paste and tomato purée.

10. Stir in cream and sauté it for 8-10 minutes. Then add the chicken escalopes to the curry. Cook till the curry reduces to half and the escalopes are done.

11. Place the escalopes on the serving platter and pour the sauce on top.

12. Serve hot, garnished with slivered almonds, garam masala and cream.

Chicken in a Spicy Spinach Puree

Serves: 4-5   Preparation time: 10 minutes   Cooking time: 45 minutes

Ingredients:

Chicken, skinned and cut .... *1 kg*
Oil .... *60 ml / 4 tbs*
Cinnamon (*daalchini*) sticks *4*
Bay leaves (*tej patta*) *2*
Ginger paste (page 10) .... *40 gms / 2 2/3 tbs*
Garlic paste (page 10) .... *40 gms / 2 2/3 tbs*
Onion paste (page 10) .... *200 gms / 1 cup*
Red chilli powder .... *10 gms / 2 tsp*
Tomatoes, chopped .... *180 gms / 3/4 cup*

Spinach (*palak*), puréed   *350 gms / 1 3/4 cups*
Maize flour (*makke ka atta*) .... *3 gms / 2/3 tsp*
Water .... *40 ml / 2 2/3 tbs*
Butter .... *100 gms / 1/2 cup*
Salt to taste
White pepper powder .... *3 gms / 2/3 tsp*
Ginger, julienned .... *10 gms / 2 tsp*
Fenugreek powder (*kasoori
methi*) .... *3 gms / 2/3 tsp*

Method:

1. Heat oil in a pan, add cinnamon and bay leaves, sauté over medium heat until they crackle.

2. Add the ginger-garlic-onion pastes and red chilli powder, and sauté for 30-60 seconds.

3. Add tomatoes and sauté further for 1 minute.

4. Add the spinach purée, stir in maize flour diluted with water and cook over medium heat for 10-15 minutes, stirring occasionally.

5. In another pan, heat butter and sauté the chicken until lightly browned.

6. Transfer the chicken pieces into the spinach purée. Add salt and white pepper powder, cover and simmer on very low heat (*dum*) for 10-15 minutes or till chicken is cooked.

7. Serve hot, garnished with julienned ginger and fenugreek powder, accompanied by any Indian bread.

Chicken with Black Pepper

Serves: 4   Preparation time: 2 hours   Cooking time: 40 minutes

Ingredients:

Chicken drumstick .... *800 gms*
Ginger paste (page 10) .... *10 gms / 2 tsp*
Garlic paste (page 10) .... *10 gms / 2 tsp*
Turmeric (*haldi*) powder .... *2 gms / ½ tsp*
Red chilli paste .... *10 gms / 2 tsp*
Salt to taste

Oil for frying
Black peppercorn, crushed ...... *10 gms / 2 tsp*
Lemon juice .... *50 ml / 3 ¹/₃ tbs*
Salt to taste
Green coriander, chopped .... *20 gms / 4 tsp*
Garam masala (page 10) .... *3 gms / ½ tsp*

Method:

1. **For the marinade**, mix together the ginger and garlic pastes, turmeric, red chilli paste and salt.

2. Marinate the chicken drumsticks in this mixture and keep aside for 2 hours.

3. Heat oil in a pan and fry chicken till golden brown in colour, remove and keep aside.

4. In a *kadhai* (wok), add chicken alongwith marinade and all other ingredients, stir-fry till chicken is fully cooked. Serve hot, accompanied by any Indian bread.

◀ *Chicken with Black Pepper*

Chicken Jalfrezi

Serves:4   Preparation time: 2½ hours   Cooking time: 35-40 minutes

Ingredients:

Chicken, boneless .... *800 gms*
Oil for frying
Onion paste (page 10) .... *100 gms / ½ cup*
Tomato purée .... *100 gms / ½ cup*
Ginger paste (page 10) .... *50 gms / 3 ²/₃ tbs*
Garlic paste (page 10) .... *50 gms / 3 ²/₃ tbs*

Salt to taste
Onion, diced .... *50 gms*
Tomato, diced .... *50 gms*
Capsicum, diced .... *50 gms*
Garam masala (page 10) .... *10 gms / 2 tsp*

Method:

1. Cut the chicken into pieces.

2. Heat oil (1 tbs) in a *kadhai* (wok). Add onion paste, cook for 5-7 minutes, then add tomato purée and cook for 10-15 minutes. Remove from heat, set aside.

3. Marinate the chicken pieces with salt and ginger-garlic pastes for 2 hours.

4. In a separate *kadhai* (wok) heat oil and add the onion, tomato mixture, add the marinated chicken and stir-fry till chicken is cooked.

5. Serve hot, accompanied by a green salad and any Indian bread.

◀ *Chicken Jalfrezi*

Kadhai Chicken

Serves: 4   Preparation time: 30 minutes   Cooking time: 30 minutes

Ingredients:

Chicken (cut into 12 pieces) .... *1 kg*
Oil .... *100 ml / ½ cup*
Garlic paste (page 10) .... *20 gms / 4 tsp*
Red chilli, pounded coarsely *6-8*
Tomatoes, blanched and chopped .... *1 kg*
Ginger, chopped .... *50 gms / 3 ²/₃ tbs*
Green chillies, sliced *2*
Salt to taste
Red and Green Bell peppers *100 gms / ½ cup*
Garam masala (page 10) .... *5 gms / 1 tsp*

Method:

1. Heat oil in a *kadhai* (wok), sauté garlic paste and red chillies, add tomatoes and cook for 5 minutes, stirring constantly. Add ginger, sliced green chillies and salt, cook on medium heat for 3-5 minutes.
2. Add chicken pieces and cook till the curry becomes thick and the chicken is tender.
3. Stir in the red-green peppers and garam masala. Cover and cook for 5-7 minutes. Serve hot, accompanied by any Indian bread.

Stir-fried Chicken

Serves: 4-5   Preparation time: 5 hours   Cooking time: 20 minutes

Ingredients:

Chicken, shredded .... *1 kg*
Ginger paste (page 10) .... *50 gms / 3 ²/₃ tbs*
Garlic paste (page 10) ....*50 gms / 3 ²/₃ tbs*
Red chilli powder ....*2.5 gms / ½ tsp*
Salt to taste
Oil .... *100 ml / ½ cup*
Water/Chicken stock .... *100 ml / ½ cup*
Red and Green chillies (slit in half) *10*
Spring onions, chopped
 in rounds ....*200 gms / 1 cup*
Black pepper powder .... *5 gms / 1 tsp*
Lemon juice ....*30 ml / 2 tbs*

Method:

1. Mix together ginger-garlic pastes, red chilli powder, salt and oil (1 tbs). Add the chicken to marinade and chill in refrigerator for 4-5 hrs.
2. Heat oil in a *kadhai* (wok) and stir-fry the chicken on high heat for 7-10 min.
3. Stir in chicken stock/water and continue stirring. Add red-green chillies and spring onions. Stir and cook for another 3-5 minutes on medium heat.
4. Stir in the black pepper and lemon juice. Cook for another 1 minute, remove from heat and serve hot, garnished with chopped coriander and accompanied by Naan (page 75).

◀ *Kadhai Chicken*

Chicken flavoured with Cashewnuts

Serves: 4-5   Preparation time: 15 minutes   Cooking time: 45 minutes

Ingredients:

Chicken, skinned and cut into 8 pieces   *1 kg*
Oil .... *80 ml / 5 1/3 tbs*
Bay leaves (*tej patta*) *2*
Cinnamon (*daalchini*) sticks (1 cm) *3*
Green cardamoms (*choti elaichi*) *8*
Black cumin (*shah jeera*) .... *3 gms / 2/3 tsp*
Cloves (*laung*) *8*
Onions, chopped .... *200 gms / 1 cup*
Turmeric (*haldi*) powder .... *6 gms / 1 1/3 tsp*
Yellow chilli powder .... *8 gms / 1 2/3 tsp*
Ginger paste (page 10) .... *25 gms / 5 tsp*

Garlic paste (page 10) .... *25 gms / 5 tsp*
Cashewnut paste .... *100 gms / 1/2 cup*
Yoghurt, whisked .... *150 gms / 3/4 cup*
Water, hot .... *200 ml / 1 cup*
Salt to taste
Cream .... *40 ml / 2 2/3 tbs*
Black cardamom (*bari elaichi*)
powder .... *3 gms / 2/3 tsp*
Eggs, soft boiled and quartered *3*
Green coriander, chopped .... *15 gms / 1 tbs*
Ginger, julienned .... *5 gms / 1 tsp*

Method:

1. Heat oil in a heavy bottomed pan over medium heat. Add bay leaves, cinnamon sticks, green cardamoms, black cumin and cloves, sauté until they begin to crackle.

2. Add onions, turmeric powder and yellow chilli powder and sauté for 30 seconds.

3. Add ginger, garlic and cashewnut pastes and sauté further for 30 seconds.

4. Add chicken pieces and cook for 10-15 minutes over medium heat.

5. Pour in the whisked yoghurt alongwith hot water and salt. Cover and simmer for 10-15 minutes on a very low heat.

6. Add the cream and cardamom powder and stir-fry for 4-5 minutes. Remove from heat.

7. Serve hot, garnished with the eggs, green coriander and julienned ginger, accompanied by Chappatis (page 75) or Naan (page 75).

LAMB

Minced Lamb with Peas (*recipe on following page*) ▶

Minced Lamb with Peas

Serves:4   Preparation time: 20 minutes   Cooking time: 40-50 minutes

Ingredients:

Lamb (minced) .... *600 gms*
Oil for frying
Onion, chopped .... *75 gms / 5 tbs*
Tomatoes, chopped .... *75 gms / 5 tbs*
Bayleaf (*tej patta*) .... *2 gms / ½ tsp*
Peppercorns .... *2 gms / ½ tsp*
Cloves (*laung*) .... *2 gms / ½ tsp*
Black cardamoms (*bari elaichi*) *2 gms / ½ tsp*
Green cardamoms (*choti elaichi*) ....
.... *2 gms / ½ tsp*

Coriander powder .... *10 gms / 2 tsp*
Cumin (*jeera*) powder .... *10 gms / 2 tsp*
Red chilli powder .... *50 gms / 2 ⅔ tbs*
Garam masala (page 10) .... *10 gms / 2 tsp*
Green coriander, chopped .... *10 gms / 2 tsp*
Salt to taste
Ginger, julienned .... *10 gms / 2 tsp*
Ginger paste (page 10) .... *50 gms / 2 ⅔ tbs*
Garlic paste (page 10) .... *50 gms / 2 ⅔ tbs*
Green peas, boiled .... *100 gms / ½ cup*

Method:

1. Heat oil in a *kadhai* (wok), sauté onions till transparent, add tomatoes and cook for 10-15 minutes, remove from heat.

2. Heat oil in a separate *kadhai* (wok), add bayleaf, peppercorns, cloves and both cardamoms, sauté till they begin to crackle.

3. Pour in the onion-tomato mixture and then add minced lamb to it. Cook for 10-15 minutes.

4. Add the remaining ingredients and cook till oil separates.

5. Add green peas and cook for another 10-15 minutes.

6. Remove from heat and serve hot, accompanied by any curry preparation and steamed rice.

◀ *Picture on preceding page*

Lamb Curry

Serves: 4-5   Preparation time: 15 minutes   Cooking time: 45 minutes

Ingredients:

Lamb .... *1 kg*
Mustard oil .... *150 ml / ¾ cup*
Onions, sliced ....*250 gms / 1¼ cups*
Onions, chopped ....*250 gms / 1¼ cups*
Green cardamoms (*choti elaichi*) *10*
Cloves (*laung*) *10*
Cinnamon (*daalchini*) sticks *4*
Black peppercorns *20*
Bay leaves (*tej patta*) *2*
Coriander powder ....*20 gms / 4 tsp*
Red chillies, whole .... *10 gms / 8*
Turmeric (*haldi*) powder .... *10 gms / 2 tsp*
Ginger paste (page 10) .... *5 gms / 1 tsp*

Garlic paste (page 10) ....*5 gms / 1 tsp*
Salt to taste
Yoghurt, whisked .... *200 ml / 1 cup*
Flour .... *4 gms / ¾ tsp*
Gramflour (*besan*) .... *4 gms / ¾ tsp*
Garam masala (page 10) .... *10 gms / 2 tsp*
Fennel (*saunf*) powder .... *4 gms / ¾ tsp*
Lemon juice ....*10 ml / 2 tsp*
Vetivier (*kewda*) ....*15 ml / 1 tbs*
Saffron (*kesar*) .... *1 gm*
Mace (*javitri*) powder .... *3 gms / ²/₃ tsp*
Green coriander, chopped .... *15 gms / 1 tbs*

Method:

1. Clean and cut lamb into small pieces with bone.
2. Heat oil (½ cup) in a *kadhai* (wok), add the sliced onions and sauté over medium heat until golden brown.
3. Add the lamb, chopped onions, green cardamoms, cloves, cinnamon, black pepper and bay leaves and cook until the liquid evaporates.
4. Add coriander powder, red chillies, turmeric, ginger-garlic pastes and salt, cook until the oil separates.
5. Add the yoghurt, bring to a boil, reduce to medium heat and cook for 10 minutes.
6. Add water (1 litre) and bring to a boil again. Cover and simmer, stirring occasionally, until lamb is tender.
7. Remove the lamb pieces from the curry and keep aside.
8. Heat oil (3 tbs) in a pan, add the flour and gramflour and cook over low heat, stirring constantly, until light brown. Add the curry and stir. Remove from heat.
9. Strain the curry, reheat and bring to a boil.
10. Add the lamb, garam masala, fennel powder, lemon juice, vetivier, saffron and mace powder, stir-fry for 10-15 minutes, remove from heat.
11. Serve hot, garnished with green coriander and accompanied by Chappatis (page 75).

Lamb with Spinach

Serves: 4 Preparation time: 1 hour Cooking time: 45 minutes

Ingredients:

Lamb, cut into boneless cubes......... *800 gms*
Green coriander, chopped ....*200 gms / 1 cup*
Mint (fresh)........................... *100 gms / ½ cup*
Spinach, chopped..............*300 gms / 1½ cups*
Poppy (*khus khus*) seeds ....*20 gms / 4 tsp*
Cashewnuts .... *80 gms / ⅓ tbs*
Oil .... *100 ml / ½ cup*
Green cardamom (*choti elaichi*) *8*

Cloves (*laung*) *6*
Onions paste (page 10) .... *100 gms / ½ cup*
Ginger-garlic paste (page 10) ....
.... *40 gms / ²/₃ tbs*
Tomatoes, chopped .... *125 gms / ½ cup*
Yellow chilli powder .... *15 gms / 1 tbs*
Peppercorns *10*
Salt to taste

Method:

1. Wash and clean the coriander, mint and spinach. Blanch the spinach in salted boiling water for 1½ minute. Allow to cool.

2. Blend together the spinach, mint and coriander. Keep aside.

3. Soak poppy seeds and cashewnut in hot water for 30 minutes. Blend to make a fine paste. Keep aside.

4. Heat oil in a heavy bottomed pan. Sauté cardamoms and cloves till they crackle.

5. Add onion paste, ginger-garlic pastes and stir-fry for 5-6 minutes. Add lamb cubes and stir-fry till lamb is evenly coated.

6. Add chopped tomatoes, yellow chilli powder, peppercorns and salt. Stir-fry for 2 minutes. Add water (1 cup), bring to a boil and simmer till water evaporates.

7. Add poppy seeds, cashewnut paste and the blended purée. Simmer till lamb is cooked. Season to taste and remove from fire.

8. Drizzle cream on top and serve hot, accompanied by boiled rice or any Indian bread.

Spicy Lamb Chops

Serves: 4-6   Preparation time: 30 minutes   Cooking time: 1 hour 15 minutes

Ingredients:

Lamb chops .... *1 kg*	Brown sugar .... *5 gms / 1 tsp*
Cumin (*jeera*) seeds .... *15 gms / 1 tbs*	Yoghurt .... *175 ml / ¾ cup*
Ginger, paste (page 10) .... *10 gms / 2 tsp*	Butter or Oil .... *40 ml / 2 ²/₃ tbs*
Garlic paste (page 10) .... *10 gms / 2 tsp*	Onions (medium size), chopped *2*
Green cardamom (*choti elaichi*) seeds	Green or Red chillies,
.... *3 gms / ½ tsp*	deseeded and sliced *2*
Cloves (*laung*), whole .... *2 or 3*	Salt to taste
Almonds, blanched *12*	Green coriander, chopped .... *10 gms / 2 tsp*
Sesame (*til*) seeds .... *10 gms / 2 tsp*	Saffron (optional) ....
Cayenne pepper .... *5 gms / 1 tsp*	.... few strands dissolved in 1 tsp milk

Method:

1. Blend together cumin seeds, ginger-garlic pastes, cardamom seeds, cloves, almonds, sesame seeds, cayenne pepper, sugar and yoghurt (2 tbs) to a purée, adding more yoghurt if the mixture is dry. Pour mixture into a bowl and set aside.

2. Melt butter/oil in a large *kadhai* (wok) or pan. Add onions and fry till golden brown.

3. Stir in the masala paste alongwith green or red chillies and salt, fry for five minutes stirring constantly. Add a spoonful of wsater at a time if the mixture becomes dry. Add the lamb chops and fry for 10 minutes on medium heat, turning chops frequently.

4. Beat the remaining yoghurt and saffron together, pour it into the lamb and mix well. Bring to a boil then reduce heat to very low, simmer for ½ hour.

5. Preheat oven to 150 °C (300 °F).

6. Transfer chops into a casserole and put into the oven to cook for at least 25 minutes.

7. Remove from the oven, garnish with chopped coriander. Serve at once accompanied by hot Naans (page 75).

◀ *Spicy Lamb Chops*

Lamb Cooked in Whole Spices

Serves: 4-5   Preparation time: 15 minutes   Cooking time: 45 minutes

Ingredients:

Lamb, cut into boneless cubes .... *1 kg*
Oil .... *100 ml / ½ cup*
Bay leaves (*tej patta*) *3*
Cloves (*laung*) *10*
Cinnamon (*daalchini*) sticks..........................*5*
Red chillies, whole *8*
Green cardamoms (*choti elaichi*) *10*
Onions, chopped or sliced ....*200 gms / 1 cup*
Ginger paste (page 10) ....*60 gms / 4 tbs*
Garlic paste (page 10) ....*60 gms / 4 tbs*

Yoghurt, whisked .... *200 ml / 1 cup*
Garam masala (page 10) ....*2 gms / ½ tsp*
Coriander powder .... *10 gms / 2 tsp*
Cumin (*jeera*) powder .... *6 gms /1 ²/₃ tsp*
Salt to taste
Mace (*javitri*) powder .... *3 gms / ²/₃ tsp*
Nutmeg (*jaiphal*) powder ....*a pinch*
Green chillies, whole *12*
Black pepper, crushed .... *10 gms / 2 tsp*
Fresh mint leaves, chopped   *8 gms / 1 ²/₃ tsp*

Method:

1. Heat oil in a pan. Add bay leaves, cloves, cinnamon sticks, red chillies and cardamoms, sauté over medium heat for few seconds until they begin to crackle.

2. Add the onions and sauté until soft and golden in colour. Stir in the ginger and garlic pastes, cook for 5 minutes.

3. Add the lamb, cook for 10-15 minutes over medium heat until the lamb emits a pleasant aroma, stirring continuously.

4. Mix in the yoghurt, cook for 5 minutes. Reduce heat, simmer and cook until the lamb is tender.

5. Sprinkle with garam masala, coriander powder, cumin powder, salt, mace powder, nutmeg powder and the crushed black pepper.

6. Arrange the green chillies over the cooked meat and cover the pan. Cook for 2-3 minutes. Remove from heat.

7. Serve hot, garnished with fresh mint leaves.

Lamb with a unique flavour of Pomegranate

Serves: 4-5   Preparation time: 6-12 hours   Cooking time: 45 minutes

Ingredients:

Lamb, cut into boneless cubes .... *1 kg*
Pomegranate juice ....*250 ml / 1¼ cups*
Oil .... *100 ml / ½ cup*
Bay leaves (*tej patta*) *3*
Cloves (*laung*) *10*
Cinnamon (*daalchini*) sticks........................*5*
Green cardamoms (*choti elaichi*) *10*
Onions, chopped or sliced ....*200 gms / 1 cup*
Ginger paste (page 10) .... *60 gms / 4 tbs*
Garlic paste (page 10)............... *60 gms / 4 tbs*
Red chilli powder .... *10 gms / 2 tsp*
Yoghurt .... *200 ml / 1 cup*

Garam masala (page 10)...........*2 gms / ½ tsp*
Coriander powder .... *10 gms / 2 tsp*
Cumin (*jeera*) powder .... *6 gms / 1 ⅓ tsp*
Mace (*javitri*) powder ....*3 gms / ⅔ tsp*
Nutmeg (*jaiphal*) powder ....*2 gms / ½ tsp*
Salt to taste
Black pepper, crushed .... *10 gms / 2 tsp*
Saffron (*kesar*) .... *0.5 gms*
Milk ....*30 ml / 2 tbs*
Almonds, fried ....*250 gms / 1¼ cups*
Fresh mint, chopped .... *8 gms / 1 ⅔ tsp*

Method:

1. Marinate the lamb cubes in pomegranate juice for 6-12 hours.

2. Heat oil in a pan, add bay leaves, cloves, cinnamon sticks and cardamoms and sauté over medium heat for a few seconds until they begin to crackle.

3. Add the onions, sauté until soft and golden in colour. Stir in the ginger and garlic pastes and red chilli powder, cook for 5 minutes, stirring continuously.

4. Add the marinated lamb alongwith the marinade, cook for 10-15 minutes over medium heat until a pleasant aroma comes from the lamb.

5. Stir in the yoghurt and cook for 5 minutes. Reduce heat, simmer on low heat and cook until the lamb is tender.

6. Sprinkle garam masala, coriander powder, cumin powder, mace, nutmeg, salt and crushed black pepper, cook for another 5-10 minutes, remove from heat.

7. Transfer to a serving dish, sprinkle saffron dissolved in a little milk, fried almonds and fresh mint leaves and serve hot.

Stir-fried Lamb Delight

Serves: 3-4   Preparation time: 15 minutes   Cooking time: 25 minutes

Ingredients:

Lamb pieces .... *600 gms*
Ginger, crushed .... *10 gms / 2 tsp*
Garlic, crushed......................... *15 gms / 1 tbs*
Salt to taste
Black cardamom (*bari elaichi*) *3*
Cinnamon (*daalchini*) *3*
Cloves (*laung*) *4*

Oil .... *80 ml / ¾ cup*
Coriander powder .... *20 gms / 4 tsp*
Red chilli powder .... *10 gms / 2 tsp*
Turmeric (*haldi*) powder ....*3 gms / ½ tsp*
Tomato, chopped..*1*
Coconut dices .... *50 gms / 3 tbs*

Method:

1. Boil lamb in water (100 ml), in a heavy bottomed *kadhai* (wok) alongwith crushed ginger, garlic, salt, black cardamom, cinnamom and cloves.

2. Cook until the lamb becomes tender. Remove and keep aside.

3. Heat oil in a *kadhai* (wok), add the cooked lamb alongwith coriander, red chilli and turmeric powder.

4. Stir-fry for 3 minutes. Add chopped tomato and coconut dices.

5. Cook further for 7-10 minutes.

6. Remove from heat and serve hot, accompanied by any Indian bread.

◀ *Stir-fried Lamb Delight*

Exotic Lamb Curry

Serves: 4-5   Preparation time: 15 minutes   Cooking time: 1 hour

Ingredients:

Lamb, boneless cubes .... *1 kg*
Oil ....*200 gms / 1 cup*
Cinnamon (*daalchini*) sticks.........................*4*
Green cardamoms (*choti elaichi*) *6*
Cloves (*laung*) *8*
Bay leaf (*tej patta*) *1*
Ginger paste (page 10) .... *50 gms / 3 1/3 tbs*
Garlic paste (page 10) .... *50 gms / 3 1/3 tbs*

Green chilli paste (page 10) *50 gms / 3 1/3 tbs*
Yoghurt, whisked .... *100 ml / 1/2 cup*
Cashewnut paste ....*300 gms / 1 1/2 cups*
Salt to taste
Black pepper ....*2 gms / 1/2 tsp*
Saffron (*kesar*) .... *2 gms*
Egg, boiled *1*

Method:

1. Heat oil in a *kadhai* (wok). Add the cinnamon, cardamoms, cloves and bay leaf and sauté over medium heat for 30 seconds, untill they begin to crackle.

2. Stir in the ginger, garlic and green chilli pastes. Cook for 10-15 minutes.

3. Add the yoghurt and lamb cubes and cook on a low fire for 45 minutes.

4. When meat is tender, add the cashewnut paste, salt, pepper and saffron. Stir briefly and remove from heat.

5. Serve hot, garnished with a boiled egg.

Note: For **Chicken Curry**, substitute lamb with chicken.

SEAFOOD

Prawn Curry (recipe on following page) ▶

Prawn Curry

Serves: 4   Preparation time: 45 minutes   Cooking time: 35 minutes

Ingredients:

Prawns, cleaned and deveined .... *1 kg*
Oil .... *100 ml / ½ cup*
Onion, finely chopped.....................................*1*
Garlic paste (page 10) .... *5 gms / 1 tsp*
Cloves (*laung*), ground .... *5 gms / 1 tsp*
Flour .... *5 gms / 1 tsp*
Turmeric (*haldi*) powder .... *5 gms / 1 tsp*

Red chilli powder .... *10 gms / 2 tsp*
Sugar .... *5 gms / 1 tsp*
Cinnamon (*daalchini*), ground   *5 gms / 1 tsp*
Beef/Chicken stock .... *150 ml / ¾ cup*
Creamed coconut................. *100 gms / ½ cup*
Lemon juice .... *5 ml / 1 tsp*
Salt to taste

Method:

1. Heat oil, sauté onion, garlic paste and cloves. Fry lightly, add flour, turmeric, chilli powder, sugar and cinnamon. Cook for a few minutes.
2. Gradually add stock and creamed coconut to the pan and bring to a boil, stirring constantly. Reduce heat and simmer for 10 minutes.
3. Add the prawns and lemon juice. Season to taste with salt, cook for another ten minutes.
4. Serve hot, garnished with julienned ginger and chopped coriander, accompanied by any Indian bread.

Shrimp with Mangoes

Serves: 4   Preparation time: 1½ hours   Cooking time: 30 minutes

Ingredients:

Shrimps .... *400 gms*
Turmeric (*haldi*) powder ....*2 gms / ½ tsp*
Salt to taste
Oil .... *80 ml / ½ cup*
Mustard (*raee*) seeds .... *5 gms / 1 tsp*
Curry leaves *4*
Onions, chopped .... *100 gms / ½ cup*

Green chilli, slit *2*
Ginger, chopped .... *15 gms / 1 tbs*
Garlic, chopped .... *15 gms / 1 tbs*
Coriander powder .... *15 gms / 1 tbs*
Red chilli powder .... *10 gms / 2 tsp*
Mangoes, raw, sliced ....*200 gms / 1 cup*
Coconut milk .... *200 ml / 1 cup*

◀ *Prawn Curry (**picture on preceding page**)*

Method:
1. Marinate shrimps in turmeric powder and salt, keep aside.
2. Heat oil in a *kadhai* (wok). Sauté shrimps. Remove and keep aside.
3. Add mustard seeds and let it crackle.
4. In the same oil, add curry leaves, onions, green chilli, ginger and garlic. Cook till onions are lightly browned. Add coriander powder, red chilli powder and stir.
5. Mix the shrimps and mangoes into the curry, add the coconut milk, cook for 15-20 minutes till the curry thickens. Remove from heat.
6. Serve hot, accompanied by steamed rice and Mixed Vegetable Raita (page 79).

Sesame Seed coated Prawns

Serves: 4-5   Preparation time: 1½ hours   Cooking time: 20 minutes

Ingredients:

Prawns (large) 8	Cheddar cheese .... *15 gms / 1 tbs*
Lemon juice ....*5 ml / 1 tsp*	Cinnamon (*daalchini*) powder *5 gms / 1 tsp*
Ginger paste (page 10) .... *10 gms / 2 tsp*	Clove (*laung*) powder .... *5 gms / 1 tsp*
Garlic paste (page 10) .... *10 gms / 2 tsp*	Fenugreek (*kasoori methi*) .... *5 gms / 1 tsp*
Salt to taste	Green chillies, chopped 6
Sesame (*til*) seeds .... *15 gms / 1 tbs*	White pepper powder .... *5 gms / 1 tsp*
Yoghurt ....*20 ml / 4 tsp*	Chaat masala .... *5 gms / 1 tsp*

Method:

1. Marinate the prawns with lemon juice, ginger-garlic pastes and salt, keep aside for half an hour.
2. Roast the sesame seeds slightly and crush them to a powder.
3. Beat yoghurt in a bowl, add the remaining ingredients (except for chaat masala and lemon juice).
4. Rub this mixture into each prawn and keep in a cool place for 1 hour.
5. Preheat the oven to 150 ºC (300 ºF).
6. Skewer the prawns and roast in the oven till light golden in colour.
7. Press the sesame seed powder over the prawns and roast again for 2 minutes.
8. Sprinkle chaat masala and serve immediately, garnished with onion rings and accompanied by a green salad.

Shrimps in Coconut

Serves: 3-4   Preparation time: 25 minutes   Cooking time: 40-50 minutes

Ingredients:

Shrimps, peeled	600 gms	Coriander powder	6 gms / 1 tsp
Oil	80 ml / 5 ⅓ tbs	Red chilli powder	5 gms / 1 tsp
Mustard (raee) seeds	3 gms / ½ tsp	Turmeric (haldi) powder	3 gms / ½ tsp
Curry leaves	2	Coconut (fresh), grated	1
Garlic, slivered	10 gms / 2 tsp	Cumin (jeera), whole	10 gms / 2 tsp
Onions, chopped	4	Salt to taste	
Green chilli, chopped	1	Coconut milk	200 ml / 1 cup

Method:

1. Heat oil in a *kadhai* (wok), sauté mustard seeds till they crackle, add curry leaves, garlic slivers and chopped onions. Stir-fry till onions are transparent.

2. Stir in all other ingredients except for coconut milk. Cook till the oil separates and appears on the surface. Add water as and when necessary to cook the curry.

3. Add coconut milk alongwith shrimps, stir-fry till shrimps are cooked and curry thickens. Remove from heat.

4. Serve hot, accompanied by Chappatis (page 75).

◀ *Shrimps in Coconut*

Pickled Prawns

Serves: 4   Preparation time: Cooking time:

Ingredients:

Prawn (medium size), peeled .... *600 gms*
Ginger paste (page 10) .... *50 gms / 3 2/3 tbs*
Garlic paste (page 10) .... *50 gms / 3 2/3 tbs*
Salt to taste
Lemon juice .... *45 ml / 3 tbs*
Mustard oil for frying
Onion (*kalonji*) seeds .... *2 gms / 1/2 tsp*
Mustard (*raee*) seeds .... *2 gms / 1/2 tsp*
Fenugreek (*methidana*) seeds *2 gms / 1/2 tsp*
Whole red chillies *4*
Coriander seeds .... *2 gms / 1/2 tsp*

Onion, sliced .... *150 gms / 3/4 cup*
Tomato, chopped .... *100 gms / 1/2 cup*
Green chillies, chopped .... *5 gms / 1 tsp*
Coriander powder .... *2 gms / 1/2 tsp*
Red chilli powder to taste
Cumin (*jeera*) powder .... *2 gms / 1/2 tsp*
Garam masala (page 10) .... *2 gms / 1/2 tsp*
Turmeric (*haldi*) powder .... *2 gms / 1/2 tsp*
Ginger, julienned .... *10 gms / 2 tsp*
Green coriander, chopped .... *25 gms / 5 tsp*

Method:

1. Mix together half of the ginger-garlic pastes, salt and lemon juice. Marinate the prawns in the mixture and keep aside for 1/2 hour.

2. Heat oil in a *kadhai* (wok), add the whole spices and sauté till they crackle.

3. Add the sliced onion, sauté till transparent, add tomatoes, green chillies and half of the coriander powder, stir-fry for 5-10 minutes.

4. To this, add salt to taste, red chilli powder, remaining coriander powder, cumin powder, garam masala, turmeric powder, stir-fry for another 5-10 minutes, add the marinated prawn and stir-fry till cooked. Add julienned ginger and chopped coriander, stir.

   Remove from heat.

5. Serve hot, garnished with green coriander and accompanied by any Indian bread.

Tomato Fish

Serves: 4   Preparation time: 30 minutes   Cooking time: 20-25 minutes

Ingredients:

Fish fillets (firm and white),
deboned and cubed.................................. *1 kg*
Turmeric (*haldi*) powder .... *10 gms / 2 tsp*
Salt to taste
Oil .... *50 ml / ¼ cup*
Onions (medium), sliced *2*
Red chilli powder .... *5 gms / 1 tsp*
Sugar .... *5 gms / 1 tsp*

Garam masala (page 10) .... *10 gms / 2 tsp*
Coriander powder .... *15 gms / 1 tbs*
Tomatoes, blanched, deseeded
and chopped .... *½ kg*
Sour cream .... *30 gms / 2 tbs*
Lemon juice .... *15 ml / 1 tbs*
Green chillies, slit in half, deseeded *4*

Method:

1. Marinate the fish cubes with turmeric powder (1½ tsp) and salt to taste. Set aside.

2. Heat oil in a deep pan, fry the fish cubes until they are evenly browned. Put
   aside on a plate.

3. Add onions and sauté till transparent. Stir in red chilli powder, sugar, garam masala,
   coriander powder and the remaining turmeric powder. Cook for 2 minutes.

4. Add tomatoes, sour cream, lemon juice, green chillies, bring to a boil, stirring
   continuously.

5. Add fried fish cubes to the sauce and coat evenly. Simmer for 10 minutes or
   until fish is cooked.

6. Serve hot, accompanied by any Indian bread.

Coconut Fish

Serves: 4-5   Preparation time: 45 minutes   Cooking time: 15 minutes

Ingredients:

Fish fillets .... *1 kg*
Malt vinegar .... *90 ml / 1/3 cup*
Lemon juice .... *25 ml / 5 tsp*
Salt to taste
For the green coconut chutney:
Coriander seeds .... *50 gms / 3 1/3 tbs*
Cumin (*jeera*) seeds .... *15 gms / 1 tbs*

Coconut (fresh), grated .... *100 gms / 1/2 cup*
Garlic paste (page 10) .... *20 gms / 1 tbs*
Green chillies, chopped *6*
Green coriander, chopped .... *15 gms / 1 tbs*
Red chilli powder .... *5 gms / 1 tsp*
Sugar .... *25 gms / 5 tsp*
Oil .... *30 ml / 2 tbs*

Method:

1. Marinate the fish fillets in vinegar, lemon juice and salt for 30 minutes.
2. Combine all the ingredients for the green chutney with a little water in a blender to make a fine paste.
3. Apply this paste evenly on the fish fillets.
4. Wrap each fillet separately in a greased piece of aluminium foil.
5. Place each wrapped fish in a steamer and steam for 10-15 minutes.
6. Unwrap the fish, arrange on a platter and serve with lemon wedges.

Fish Fillets in Coconut Sauce

Serves: 4   Preparation time: 10-15 minutes   Cooking time: 30-40 minutes

Ingredients:

Fish-fillets—sole or plain, cut into 3 pieces *4*
Oil .... *30 ml / 2 tbs*
Onion (*kalonji*) seeds .... *5 gms / 1 tsp*
Red chillies (whole), dried *4*
Garlic cloves, sliced *3*
Onion (medium), sliced *1*
Tomatoes (medium), sliced *2*

Coconut, shredded .... *30 gms / 2 tbs*
Salt to taste
Coriander powder .... *5 gms / 1 tsp*
Water .... *150 ml / 3/4 cup*
Lime juice .... *15 ml / 1 tbs*
Coriander, chopped .... *15 gms / 1 tbs*

Method:

1. Heat oil in a *kadhai* (wok). Reduce heat and add onion seeds, dried red chillies, garlic and onion. Stir-fry for 3-4 minutes.
2. Mix in the tomatoes, grated coconut, salt and coriander.
3. Add the fish pieces to the mixture and turn gently to cook evenly.
4. Simmer and cook for 5-7 minutes.
5. Stir in the water, lime juice and chopped coriander. Cook further for 3-5 minutes or until the water evaporates.
6. Remove to serving dish and serve hot, accompanied by steamed rice and Mixed Vegetable Raita (page 79).

Fish Moilee

Serves: 4-5   Preparation time: 10-15 minutes   Cooking time: 30-40 minutes

Ingredients:

Fish fillets .... *600 gms*
Oil .... *50 ml / 3 2/3 tbs*
Green cardamom (*choti elaichi*) *6*
Curry leaves *2*
Green chillies, slit *4-5*
Ginger, chopped .... *10 gms / 2 tsp*

Garlic, chopped .... *15 gms / 1 tbs*
Onions, chopped .... *100 gms*
Turmeric (*haldi*) powder ....*3 gms / ½ tsp*
Coconut milk ....*500 ml / 2½ cups*
Salt to taste

Method:

1. Heat oil in a *kadhai* (wok), add cardamom, curry leaves, green chillies, ginger and garlic, stir-fry for a minute. Add onions, sauté till transparent.
2. Stir in turmeric, fish fillets and coconut milk, cook for 15-20 minutes.
3. Season with salt, bring to boil and simmer for 8-10 minutes or until the fish is cooked.
4. Transfer to a serving dish and serve hot, accompanied by steamed rice and green salad.

◀ *Fish Moilee*

Fish in Yoghurt

Serves: 4   Preparation: 20 minutes   Cooking: 25 minutes

Ingredients:

Pomfret fillets	700 gms	Ginger, chopped	20 gms / 4 tsp
Salt to taste		Onions, chopped	75 gms / 5 tbs
Lemon juice	45 ml / 3 tbs	Tomatoes, chopped	80 gms / 5 ^{2}/$_3$ tbs
Turmeric (haldi) powder	5 gms / 1 tsp	Red chilli powder	3 gms / ½ tsp
Oil	100 ml / ½ cup	Cumin (jeera) powder	3 gms / ½ tsp
Mustard (raee) seeds	3 gms / ½ tsp	Coriander powder	3 gms / ½ tsp
Curry leaves	10	Yoghurt, whisked	150 gms / ¾ cup

Method:

1. Marinate the pomfret fillets with half the salt, lemon juice and turmeric powder. Keep aside for 15 minutes.

2. Heat oil in a nonstick pan and fry the marinated fillets till golden brown. Drain and keep aside.

3. To the same oil, add mustard seeds and curry leaves and sauté till the seeds crackle.

4. Add chopped ginger and onions and cook till onions are soft. Add tomatoes and cook till the oil separates.

5. Stir in the red chilli, cumin and coriander powders and the remaining turmeric. Stir for 1 minute.

6. Mix in the yoghurt. Bring to boil and simmer for 7 minutes.

7. Slip the fried fish into the curry and simmer for another 4 minutes.

8. Carefully remove the fillets and place on the serving dish and pour the curry on top.

9. Serve hot, accompanied by steamed rice or Chappatis (page 75) and Mixed Vegetable Raita (page 79).

◀ *Fish in Yoghurt*

Seafood and Mixed Vegetable Bonanza

Serves: 4-5   Preparation time: 1½ hours   Cooking time: 30 minutes

Ingredients:

Cod fish, skinned, cut into cubes ..... *225 gms*
Prawns, cooked .... *225 gms*
Crab sticks, cut length ways *6*
Lemon juice .... *15 ml / 1 tbs*
Coriander powder .... *5 gms / 1 tsp*
Red chilli, powder .... *5 gms / 1 tsp*
Salt to taste
Cumin (*jeera*), ground .... *5 gms / 1 tsp*
Cornflour .... *45 gms / 3 tbs*
Oil .... *300 ml / 1½ cup*

Onions (medium), chopped *2*
Onion (*kalonji*) seeds .... *5 gms / 1 tsp*
French beans, (2 x 1 cm) .... *115 gms*
Sweetcorn .... *200 gms / 1 cup*
Ginger, shredded .... *5 gms / 1 tsp*
Salt to taste
Green chillies, sliced *4*
Red chilli powder .... *5 gms / 1 tsp*
Green coriander, chopped .... *30 gms / 2 tbs*

Method:

1. Mix together, the seafood in a bowl and keep aside.

2. Sprinkle the lemon juice, ground coriander, chilli powder, salt and cumin on the seafood and mix gently to coat evenly.

3. Sprinkle cornflour and mix to coat the seafood thoroughly. Refrigerate for one hour.

4. Heat oil (3/4 cup) in a *kadhai* (wok). Add the chopped onions alongwith onion seeds and sauté until the onion is lightly browned.

5. Stir in the french beans, sweet corn, ginger, salt, green chillies, red chilli powder and chopped coriander. Stir-fry for 7 to 10 minutes over moderate heat. Remove from heat and place on a serving platter. Keep warm.

6. Heat the remaining oil in a *kadhai* (wok), fry the marinated seafood to a golden brown colour in 2-3 batches. Remove and drain all excess oil.

7. Place the seafood alongside the prepared vegetables, garnish with lemon wedges and serve hot, accompanied by Mixed Vegetable Raita (page 79).

VEGETABLES

***Tangy Potato Dish* (recipe on following page)** ▶

Tangy Potato Dish

Serves: 3-4   Preparation time: 20 minutes   Cooking time: 30 minutes

Ingredients:

Potatoes, peeled .... *600 gms*
Mint, fresh .... *5 gms / 1 tsp*
Lemon juice .... *30 ml / 2 tbs*
Green chillies *3*
Green coriander, chopped .. *100 gms / ½ cup*
Oil .... *100 ml / ½ cup*

Ginger paste (page 10) .... *10 gms / 2 tsp*
Garlic paste (page 10) .... *10 gms / 2 tsp*
Cumin (*jeera*) powder .... *5 gms / 1 tsp*
Coriander powder .... *8 gms / 1½ tsp*
Red chilli paste .... *8 gms / 1½ tsp*
Salt to taste

Method:

1. Blend together fresh mint, lemon juice, green chillies and green coriander into a purée.
2. Heat oil in a heavy bottomed pan. Add ginger-garlic pastes and potatoes. Stir-fry for 2-3 minutes. Add cumin, coriander powder and red chilli paste. Stir-fry, add salt and water (250 ml). Bring to a boil and simmer till potatoes are cooked.
3. Add the blended purée and stir-fry for 4-5 minutes. Add salt and serve at once.

Stir-fried Peas and Potatoes

Serves: 4   Preparation time: 30 minutes   Cooking time: 45 minutes

Ingredients:

Potatoes, peeled and cubed .... *225 gms*
Peas, frozen or fresh .... *½ kg*
Oil / Clarified butter (*ghee*) ....*30 ml / 2 tbs*
Onion (medium), finely chopped *1*
Ginger, finely chopped .... *8 gms / 1½ tsp*
Garlic cloves .... *3-5 gms / ½ tsp*

Tomatoes (medium), chopped *2*
Green chilli, chopped *1*
Turmeric (*haldi*) powder .... *5 gms / 1 tsp*
Water .... *100 ml / ½ cup*
Salt to taste
Green coriander, chopped ....*30 gms / 2 tbs*

Method:

1. Heat oil, add onions and sauté, stir in ginger, garlic and green chilli. Cook for 5 minutes, stirring continuously. Add the tomatoes, cook for 2-3 minutes until tomatoes are soft. Stir in the turmeric, peas, potatoes and salt. Cover the pan and simmer for 20 minutes.
2. Add water (½ cup) to prevent the mixture from becoming dry. Stir in coriander, simmer until the vegetables are tender.
3. Serve at once, accompanied by Chappatis (page 75) or Pooris (page 76).

◀ *Tangy Potato Dish* (*picture on preceding page*)

Potato and Paneer Dumplings in Curry

Serves: 6   Preparation time: 30 minutes   Cooking time: 1 hour

Ingredients:

For the dumplings:

Potatoes, boiled and mashed *3-4*
Cottage cheese (**paneer*), grated .... *500 gms*
Green coriander, chopped .... *45 gms / 3 tbs*
Mixed nuts, finely chopped ...... *45 gms / 3 tbs*
Turmeric (*haldi*) powder ....*2 gms / ½ tsp*
Asafoetida (*heeng*) powder ....*a pinch*
Ginger, finely shredded.............. *15 gms / 1 tbs*
Green chillies, deseeded, chopped........... *1-2*
Dry mango powder (*amchoor*) *2 gms / ½ tsp*
Lemon juice ....*5 ml / 1 tsp*
Salt ....*7 gms / 1½ tsp*
Cornflour.....................................*30 gms / 2 tbs*
Oil for frying

For the curry:

Clarified butter (*ghee*) ....*75 ml / 5 tbs*
Mixed nuts, finely chopped   *40 gms / 2²/₃ tbs*
Ginger, finely chopped .... *15 gms / 1 tbs*
Green chillies, chopped *2*
Coriander powder .... *7 gms / 1½ tsp*
Cumin (*jeera*), ground .... *5 gms / 1 tsp*
Turmeric (*haldi*) powder ....*2 gms / ½ tsp*
Water ....*250 ml / 1¼ cups*
Cumin (*jeera*) seeds .... *5 gms / 1 tsp*
Cinnamon (*daalchini*) stick (1" piece) *1*
Cloves (*laung*) *4*
Tomatoes, finely chopped ... *600 gms / 3 cups*
Salt to taste

Method:

* For recipe of *paneer,* turn to page 10.

1. Knead the grated cottage cheese till it is of a smooth and creamy texture. Add the mashed potatoes, coriander, mixed nuts, turmeric powder, asafoetida powder, ginger, green chillies, dry mango powder, lemon juice, salt and cornflour, knead until the ingredients are thoroughly mixed in.
2. Lightly oil your hands and divide the mixture into 12 portions. Roll each portion into a ball. Place all the balls on a tray lined with plastic wrap and set aside.
3. Heat oil in a *kadhai* (wok) to 175 °C (350 °F). Slide in a few balls at a time and fry until golden brown on all sides. Remove, drain excess oil on paper towel and keep aside.
4. **For the curry**, process together the nuts, ginger, green chillies, coriander, cumin, turmeric powder, cumin seeds, tomatoes, salt and coriander powder, into a paste.
5. Heat clarified butter in a *kadhai* (wok), sauté cumin seeds, cinnamon stick and cloves, till they crackle. Mix in the prepared paste, water and stir-fry for 10-15 minutes.
6. Add the fried balls and cook for 10-15 minutes.
7. Remove from heat, serve hot, accompanied by Mint Raita (page 79) and steamed rice.

Pomegranate Potatoes

Serves:4   Preparation time: 30 minutes   Cooking time: 15-20 minutes

Ingredients:

Potatoes, boiled, cut into 1½" cubes .... *1 kg*
Pomegranate (*anar dana*) seeds,
dried, crushed ....*200 gms / 1 cup*
Butter .... *100 gms / ½ cup*
Coriander powder .... *15 gms / 1 tbs*

Turmeric (*haldi*) powder ....*3 gms / ½ tsp*
Red chilli powder ....*6 gms / 1 tsp*
Salt to taste
Green chillies, slit *6*
Green coriander, chopped ....*20 gms / 4 tsp*

Method:
1. Heat butter in a heavy bottomed pan. Add coriander powder, turmeric powder, red chilli powder and half of the pomegranate seeds and stir.
2. Mix in the potatoes. Sprinkle salt and green chillies. Mix gently, so the spices coat the potatoes evenly, reduce heat and simmer for 10-15 minutes. Remove from heat.
3. Serve hot, garnished with chopped coriander and remaining pomegranate seeds.

Spinach Potato Delight

Serves: 4-5   Preparation time: 25 minutes   Cooking time: 25 minutes

Ingredients:

Spinach (*palak*), finely chopped .... *1 kg*
Potatoes, boiled, cubed ... *250 gms / 1¼ cups*
Water ....*2 litres / 10 cups*
Salt to taste
Maize flour (*makke ka atta*) .... *10 gms / 2 tsp*

Clarified butter (*ghee*) .... *30 gms / 2 tbs*
Onions, chopped ....*25 gms / 5 tsp*
Ginger, chopped fine ....*25 gms / 5 tsp*
Green chillies, chopped *3*
Cream .... *10 gms / 2 tsp*

Method:
1. Boil spinach in salted water for 10 minutes, drain excess water and purée the spinach.
2. Reheat spinach purée, add potato and mix well.
3. Add maize flour slowly and cook for 10 minutes.
4. In a separate pan, heat the clarified butter and brown the onions with half the ginger. Add green chillies and sauté for 1 minute.
5. Pour this over the potato-spinach mixture, stir well and bring to a boil.
6. Serve hot, garnished with julienned ginger and cream, accompanied by Chappatis (page 75).

◀ *Pomegranate Potatoes*

Buttered Vegetables

Serves: 4 Preparation: 1 hour Cooking: 45 minutes

Ingredients:

Beans (green) .... *200 gms*
Carrots.. *200 gms*
Potatoes .... *200 gms*
Cauliflower .... *200 gms*
Green peas .... *100 gms / ½ cup*
Red pumpkin .... *200 gms*
Butter................................. *250 gms / 1¼ cups*
Ginger paste (page 10) .... *40 gms / 2 ²/₃ tbs*

Garlic paste (page 10) .... *40 gms / 2 ²/₃ tbs*
Green chillies, chopped *5*
Tomatoes, chopped .... *1 kg*
Salt to taste
Red chilli powder .... *5 gms / 1 tbs*
Cream .... *150 ml / ¾ cup*
Fenugreek (*kasoori methi*) powder ... *15 gms*
Green coriander, chopped ....*25 gms / 5 tsp*

Method:

1. Wash, peel and cut vegetables into 1 cm dices.
2. **For the curry**, melt half the butter in a heavy bottomed pan. Add ginger-garlic pastes, tomatoes, salt, red chilli powder and water (2½ cups), cover and simmer till tomatoes are mashed.
3. Cool and strain curry through a fine sieve.
4. In a *kadhai* (wok), melt remaining butter, sauté green chillies over medium heat and add vegetables. Stir for 4 minutes, pour the curry and simmer till vegetables are cooked.
5. Add cream and fenugreek alongwith salt.
6. Serve hot, topped with a whirl of cream and chopped coriander.

Spicy Bengal Gram

Serves: 4-5 Preparation time: 45 minutes Cooking time: 1 hour

Ingredients:

Bengal gram (*chana*), split *250 gms/1¼ cups*
Water .... *1.5 litres / 7½ cups*
Bay leaf (*tej patta*) *1*
Cinnamon (*daalchini*) stick *1*

Butter.................................... *40 gms / 2 ²/₃ tbs*
Onions, chopped .... *100 gms / ½ cup*
Garam masala (page 10) .... *6 gms / 1¹/₃ tsp*
Ginger paste (page 10) .... *10 gms / 2 tsp*

Garlic paste (page 10) .... *10 gms / 2 tsp*   Green coriander, chopped .... *5 gms / 1 tsp*
Tomatoes, skinned & chopped *60 gms / 4 tbs*   Salt to taste

Method:

1. Clean the gram, wash in water 3 or 4 times and soak for 30 minutes in a bowl of water.
2. Boil water in a saucepan. Add bay leaf, cinnamon stick and the drained gram, bring to a slow boil. Remove the scum from the top of the pan and simmer until the gram is completely cooked. Discard the bay leaf and cinnamon stick.
3. Heat butter in a pan and sauté the onions till they are soft and golden. Add the garam masala, ginger-garlic pastes and sauté over medium heat for 2-3 minutes.
4. Add the tomatoes, cooked gram and salt, cover and cook for 2-3 minutes.
5. Serve hot, garnished with green coriander.

Lotus Stems in an Exotic Curry

Serves: 4   Preparation time: 10 minutes   Cooking time: 30 minutes

Ingredients:

Lotus stem (*kamal kakri*) .... *800 gms*   Cumin (*jeera*) powder .... *2 gms / 1/3 tsp*
Mustard oil .... *250 ml / 1¼ cups*   Cinnamon (*daalchini*)
Water   powder .... *2 gms / 1/3 tsp*
Cloves (*laung*) .... *2*   Black cardamom (*bari*
Green cardamoms (*choti elaichi*) .... *2*   *elaichi*) powder .... *6 gms / 1 tsp*
Fennel (*saunf*) powder .... *30 gms / 2 tbs*   Yoghurt, whisked .... *1½ kg / 7½ cups*
Salt ....,................................. *5 gms / 1 tsp*

Method:

1. Scrape away the skin of the lotus stems. Cut into 1½" long pieces, discarding the ends. Wash well and drain.
2. Heat mustard oil in a *kadhai* (wok). Deep fry the lotus stems till they are half cooked. Drain excess oil and keep aside.
3. To the same *kadhai* (wok), add water and the lotus stems, bring to a boil, add all the spices, mix in the yoghurt. Cook till the curry thickens and the lotus stems are tender, stirring regularly.
4. Remove into a serving dish and serve hot, accompanied by steamed rice.

Tomato Delight

Serves: 4-5   Preparation time: 20 minutes   Cooking time: 40 minutes

Ingredients:

Tomatoes (quarters) .... *1 kg*	Salt to taste	
Oil .... *100 ml / ½ cup*	Onions (*kalonji*) seeds ....*2 gms / ½ tsp*	
Ginger paste (page 10) ....*7.5 gms / 1½ tsp*	Fenugreek (*methi dana*)	
Red chilli powder .... *10 gms / 1 tsp*	seeds .... *1.5 gms / ½ tsp*	
Coriander powder ....*8 gms / ½ tsp*	Mustard (*raee*) seeds ....*1.5 gms / ½ tsp*	
Garlic paste (page 10) ....*10 gms / 1 tsp*	Whole red chillies...*3*	
Cumin (*jeera*) powder ....*10 gms / 2 tsp*	Cherry tomatoes, blanched *20*	

Method:

1. Heat half the oil in a thick bottom *kadhai* (wok).
2. Add ginger and garlic paste. Stir-fry for a minute.
3. Add red chilli powder, coriander powder, cumin powder and salt to taste. Add tomatoes and stir-fry till tomatoes are cooked.
4. Strain and keep aside.
5. Heat remaining oil. Add onion seed, fenugreek seeds, mustard seeds and whole red chillies. Let them crackle and add to the strained sauce.
6. Add cherry tomatoes to the sauce and simmer for about 4 minutes.
7. Serve immediately, accompanied by steamed rice.

Spinach Tomato Stir-fry

Serves: 4-5   Preparation time: 10 minutes   Cooking time: 15 minutes

Ingredients:

Spinach (*palak*), fresh or frozen .... *1 kg*	Onions, sliced or chopped .. *100 gms / ½ cup*
Tomatoes, chopped.......... *250 gms / 1¼ cups*	Garlic, peeled, cut lengthwise *60 gms / 4 tbs*
Oil ....*60 ml / 4 tbs*	Red chilli powder .... *5 gms / 1 tsp*
Cumin (*jeera*) seeds .... *5 gms / 1 tsp*	Red chillies, dried, cut in half.......................*8*

◀ *Tomato Delight*

Turmeric (*haldi*) powder .... *3 gms/²/₃ tsp*	Salt to taste
Asafoetida (*heeng*) powder .... *a pinch*	Ginger, julienned .... *10 gms / 2 tsp*

Method:

1. Wash the spinach and chop roughly.

2. Heat oil in a *kadhai* (wok) to smoking point, reduce heat, add red chillies, cumin seeds, onions, garlic, red chilli powder, turmeric powder and asafoetida, stir-fry for 2-3 minutes.

3. Add chopped tomatoes and cook for 2 minutes.

4. Add the spinach, toss and stir-fry. Sprinkle salt, cover and cook over very low heat for 6-7 minutes.

5. Garnish with julienned ginger and serve hot, accompanied by Chappatis (page 75).

Stir-fried Spinach with Cottage Cheese

Serves: 4   Preparation time: 10-15 minutes   Cooking time: 25-30 minutes

Ingredients:

Spinach (*palak*) .... *1 kg*	Whole red chilli *2*
Cottage cheese (**paneer*) .... *400 gms*	Coriander powder ....*3 gms / ½ tsp*
Oil ....*60 ml / 4 tbs*	Cumin (*jeera*) powder ....*2 gms / ½ tsp*
Cumin (*jeera*) seeds ....*5 gms / 1 tsp*	Red chilli powder ....*3 gms / ½ tsp*
Garlic cloves .... *10 gms*	Salt to taste

Method:

*For recipe of *paneer*, turn to page 10.

1. Blanch spinach, drain and chop coarsely

2. Cut cottage cheese into cubes.

3. Heat oil in a *kadhai* (wok). Add cumin, garlic and sauté until garlic changes colour, add whole red chillies, stir for half a minute. Add spinach, stir-fry adding coriander powder, cumin powder and red chilli powder.

4. Add cottage cheese and stir-fry for 5 minutes. Season with salt.

5. Serve hot, accompanied by Parantha (page73) and Mixed Vegetable Raita (page 79).

◀ *Stir-fried Spinach with Cottage Cheese*

Shahi Paneer

Serves: 4-5   Preparation time: 30 minutes   Cooking time: 20 minutes

Ingredients:

Cottage cheese (*paneer*), fingers .... *1 kg*
Oil .... *80 ml / 5 1/3 tbs*
Cloves (*laung*) 6
Bay leaves (*tej patta*) 2
Cinnamon (*daalchini*) sticks.......................3
Green cardamoms (*choti elaichi*) 6
Onion paste (page 10) ....*200 gms / 1 cup*
Ginger paste (page 10) .... *40 gms / 2²/₃ tbs*
Garlic paste (page 10) .... *40 gms / 2²/₃ tbs*
Red chilli powder .... *10 gms / 2 tsp*
Turmeric (*haldi*) powder ....*4 gms / ³/₄ tsp*
Coriander powder .... *5 gms / 1 tsp*
Cashewnut paste .... *10 gms / 2 tsp*

Salt to taste
Red colouring .... *¹/₃ tsp*
Yoghurt, whisked .... *180 ml / ³/₄ cup*
Sugar .... *10 gms / 2 tsp*
Double cream .... *120 ml / ²/₃ cup*
Garam masala (page 10) .... *8 gms / 1²/₃ tsp*
Green cardamom (*choti
elaichi*) powder .... *3 gms / ²/₃ tsp*
Mace powder (*javitri*) .... *3 gms / ²/₃ tsp*
Vetivier (*kewda*) ....3 drops
Saffron (*kesar*), dissolved in 1 tbs milk ....
....*a pinch*

Method:

* For recipe of *paneer,* turn to page 10.

1. Heat oil in a pan, add cloves, bay leaves, cinnamon stick and green cardamoms, sauté over medium heat until they begin to crackle. Add onion paste and stir-fry for 2-3 minutes.

2. Stir in the ginger-garlic pastes, red chilli powder, turmeric powder, coriander powder, cashewnut paste, salt and colour.

3. Add yoghurt, warm water (½ cup) and sugar, bring to a slow boil and then simmer until the oil separates.

4. Allow the curry to cool, remove whole spices and blend to a smooth consistency.

5. Reheat the curry, stir in the cream, garam masala, cardamom powder, mace powder, vetivier and saffron.

6. Add the cottage cheese fingers, cook further for 5 minutes.

7. Serve hot, garnished with chopped coriander, accompanied by any dry vegetable preparation and Paranthas (page 73).

Stir-fried Mushrooms

Serves: 4-5   Preparation time: 10 minutes   Cooking time: 15 minutes

Ingredients:

Mushrooms, quartered .... *600 gms*
Oil .... *120 ml / 2/3 cup*
Cabbage, shredded .... *120 gms / 2/3 cup*
Red chillies, whole *4*
Coriander seeds .... *5 gms / 1 tsp*
Onions, sliced .... *80 gms / 1/3 cup*
Garlic paste (page 10) ....*20 gms / 4 tsp*

Garam masala (page 10) .... *10 gms / 2 tsp*
Salt to taste
Tomatoes, chopped .... *500 gms / 2½ cups*
Green chillies, chopped *4*
Ginger, chopped .... *30 gms / 6 tsp*
Green coriander, chopped ...... *20 gms / 4 tsp*
Capsicum, julienned ....*60 gms / 4 tbs*

Method:

1. Heat oil (2 tbs) in a *kadhai* (wok). Stir-fry the quartered mushroom over medium heat for a few minutes. Remove and keep aside.

2. In the same oil stir-fry the shredded cabbage until the liquid evaporates.

3. Pound the red chillies and coriander seeds with a pestle.

4. Heat the remaining oil in a *kadhai* (wok). Sauté the onions till they are transparent. Add the garlic paste and stir for 20 seconds over medium heat.

5. Add the pounded red chillies and coriander, garam masala and salt. Stir for 30 seconds. Add tomatoes and cook till the oil separates.

6. Add the green chillies, ginger and half the green coriander and stir. Add the stir-fried mushroom and cabbage and cook for a few minutes.

7. Garnish with julienned capsicum and the remaining green coriander. Serve hot, accompanied by steamed rice or Chappatis (page 71).

Mushroom and Corn Bonanza

Serves: 4-6   Preparation time: 15 minutes   Cooking time: 30 minutes

Ingredients:

Mushroom .... *500 gms*
Sweet Corn .... *250 gms*
Oil .... *80 ml / 5 1/3 tbs*
Green cardamoms (*choti elaichi*) *4*
Cloves (*laung*) *3*
Ginger paste (page 10) .... *10 gms / 2 tsp*
Garlic paste (page 10) .... *10 gms / 2 tsp*
Mace (*javitri*) powder .... *a pinch*

Onion paste (page 10) .... *100 gms / ½ cup*
Cashewnut paste .... *50 gms / 3 1/3 tbs*
Yoghurt .... *250 gms / 1¼ cup*
Green chilli, slit *4*
Salt to taste
Cream .... *100 ml / ½ cup*
Green coriander, chopped   *50 gms / 3 2/3 tbs*

Method:

1. Heat oil in a heavy bottomed pan.
2. Add green cardamom, cloves and mace powder. As it crackles, add ginger
    and garlic pastes.
3. Stir-fry for few minutes. Add onion paste and cashew paste.
4. Stir-fry for 5-6 minutes. Add yogurt, slit green chillies and salt.
5. Add mushroom and corn, simmer for 20 minutes.
6. Stir in the cream, garnish with slit green chillies and serve at once, accompanied by
    Masala Poori (page 72).

Mushroom Masala

Serves: 4   Preparation time: 10 minutes   Cooking time: 20 minutes

Ingredients:

Mushrooms .... ½ kg	Turmeric (*haldi*) powder ....*3 gms / ½ tsp*
Oil .... *22 ml / 4½ tsp*	Garam masala (page 10) ....*3 gms / ½ tsp*
Onions, sliced *2*	Red chilli powder ....*3 gms/ ½ tsp*
Garlic paste (page 10) .... *5 gms / 1 tsp*	Salt to taste
Tomato, chopped..*1*	Green coriander, chopped .... *15 gms / 1 tbs*

Method:

1. Cut mushrooms in slices.

2. Heat oil in a *kadhai* (wok) and fry onions until golden in colour.

3. Add garlic paste and chopped tomatoes, mix well.

4. Mix in turmeric powder, garam masala, red chilli powder and salt, fry for 3-4 minutes.

5. Stir in mushrooms and simmer until mushrooms are tender, adding very little water if necessary.

6. Garnish with chopped coriander and serve hot, accompanied by any curry dish and Chappatis (page 75).

◀ *Mushroom Masala*

Beans Poriyal

Serves: 4-5   Preparation time: 25 minutes   Cooking time: 20 minutes

Ingredients:

Beans .... *1 kg*	Red chillies, whole 2
Turmeric (*haldi*) powder ....*2 gms / ½ tsp*	Onion, chopped 2
Salt ....*5 gms / 1 tsp*	Green chillies, chopped 2
Oil ....*60 ml / 4 tbs*	Salt to taste
Mustard (*raee*) seeds ....*5 gms / 1 tsp*	Coconut (fresh), grated .... ½
Lentils (*dhuli urad daal*) ....*5 gms / 1 tsp*	

Method:

1. Remove the strings from the beans and chop finely.

2. Boil beans in water (1 cup) adding turmeric powder and salt, cook until beans are almost done. Drain excess water and keep aside.

3. Heat oil in a *kadhai* (wok). Add mustard seeds, lentils and whole red chillies. When mustard seeds begin to crackle, add chopped onions and green chillies.

4. Stir-fry for 4-5 minutes.

5. Add beans and stir-fry till beans are cooked.

6. Add salt to taste and the grated coconut, stir and remove from fire.

7. Serve immediately accompanied by a curry dish and steamed rice or Parathas (page 73).

◀ *Beans Poriyal*

Gramflour Dumplings in a Tangy Yoghurt Curry

Serves: 4　　　　　　　Preparation: 45 minutes　　　　Cooking: 30 minutes

Ingredients

Gramflour (*besan*) .... *120 gm / ½ cup*
Yoghurt .... *360 gm / 1½ cups*
Salt to taste
Red chilli powder ....*5 gm / 1 tsp*
Turmeric (*haldi*) powder ....*5 gm / 1 tsp*
Soda bi-carb ....*a pinch*
Carom (*ajwain*) seeds .... *2.5 gm / ½ tsp*
Oil to deep fry
Groundnut oil ....*60 ml / 4 tbs*

Green chillies, chopped *5*
Potatoes, cut round .... *150 gm*
Onion rounds (¼ " thick) .... *150 gm*
Cumin (*jeera*) seeds .... *2.5 gm / ½ tsp*
Mustard (*raee*) seeds .... *1.25 gm / ¼ tsp*
Fenugreek (*methi dana*)
seeds .... *1.25 gm / ¼ tsp*
Red chillies, whole *4*

Method:

1. Whisk yoghurt, salt, red chilli powder, turmeric powder and half the gramflour together in a bowl. Keep aside.
2. Sieve the other half of the gramflour and soda bi-carb together, add the carom seeds and mix enough water to make a thick batter. Beat well. Add green chillies.
3. Heat enough oil in a *kadhai* (wok) to deep fry. Drop large spoonfuls of batter in the oil to get 1½ inch puffy dumplings.
4. Fry till golden brown on both sides. Remove and keep aside.
5. Heat the groundnut oil (3 tbs) in a *handi* (pot), add the yoghurt mixture and water (3 cups). Bring to a boil, reduce heat and simmer for 8-10 minutes, stirring constantly to avoid the yoghurt from curdling.
6. Add the potatoes and onions and cook till potatoes are done.
7. Add the dumplings and simmer for 3 minutes.
8. Heat the remaining oil (1 tbs) in a small frying pan. Add the cumin, mustard and fenugreek seeds and sauté till the cumin crackles. Add the whole red chillies. Stir.
9. Pour this tempering over the simmering hot *kadhi*.
10. Remove to a bowl and serve hot, accompanied by boiled rice.

ACCOMPANIMENTS & DESSERTS

Masala Poori (recipe on following page) ▶

Masala Poori

Serves: 16   Preparation time: 15 minutes + 3 hours   Cooking time: ½ hour
(for dough resting)

Ingredients:

Flour, sieved .... *400 gms / 2 cups*	Cumin (*jeera*) powder .... *10 gms / 2 tsp*
Salt ....*2 gms / ½ tsp*	Coriander powder .... *10 gms / 2 tsp*
Cayenne pepper or Paprika ....*a pinch*	Oil .... *30 ml / 2 tbs + for frying*
Turmeric (*haldi*) powder ....*a pinch*	

Method:

1. Mix the flour, salt, cayenne pepper, turmeric, coriander and cumin. Add oil and rub it in till it is thoroughly incorporated. Add water, knead into a medium soft dough.
2. Lightly oil your palms and knead until the dough is silky smooth and pliable. Shape into a smooth ball. Brush with oil and keep aside for 3 hours.
3. Knead again briefly, divide into 16 equal portions and shape into balls.
4. Compress each into a 2" patty. Dip one end of the patty in oil and roll out into a 5" round, place on a flat surface. Similarly, roll out the other portions.
5. Heat oil in a *kadhai* (wok). Carefully slip one round into the hot oil. Fry until it puffs up and is golden brown on both sides. Remove and drain on paper towels.
6. Serve hot, as an accompaniment to any curry dish.

Bhatura

Serves: 4-5   Preparation time: 1 hour   Cooking time: 20 minutes

Ingredients:

Flour .... *400 gms / 2 cups*	Yoghurt ....*25 gms / 5 tsp*
Semolina (*sooji*) .... *100 gms / ½ cup*	Sugar ....*10 gms / 2 tsp*
Baking powder.......................... *3 gms / ⅔ tsp*	Water .... *150 ml / ¾ cup*
Baking soda ....*a pinch*	Clarified butter (*ghee*) ....*20 gms / 4 tsp*
Salt to taste	Oil for deep frying ....*500 ml / 2½ cups*

◀ *Masala Poori* (**picture on preceding page**)

Method:

1. Sieve the flour, semolina, baking powder, baking soda and salt into a bowl.

2. Whisk the yoghurt and sugar together, add to the flour, mix in cold water and knead. Cover the bowl and keep aside for 20 minutes.

3. Add clarified butter to the dough and knead to make a fine, soft dough. Cover and set aside for 30 minutes.

4. Divide into 20 equal balls, roll out each ball and pull gently from both ends to make an oval shape.

5. Heat oil in a *kadhai* (wok). Deep fry each *bhatura* untill it is golden brown on both sides.

6. Serve hot, as an accompaniment to any curry dish.

Parantha

Serves: 4-5   Preparation time: 20 minutes   Cooking time: 10 minutes

Ingredients:

Whole wheat flour ....*500 gms / 2½ cups*   Clarified butter (*ghee*) ....*200 gms / 1 cup*
Salt to taste   Water ....*250 ml / 1¼ cups*

Method:

1. Sieve the flour and salt in a bowl, incorporate melted clarified butter (2 tbs), add water gradually and knead to a smooth dough.

2. Divide into 5 equal portions and shape into balls. Dust with flour, cover and keep aside for 10 minutes.

3. Flatten each ball of dough and roll out. Brush with clarified butter and fold over. Brush the folded surface with clarified butter and fold over again to form a triangle. Roll out the triangle with a rolling pin.

4. Heat a *tawa* (griddle) and brush the surface with clarified butter. Place the *parantha* on the *tawa* and cook for a few minutes. Coat with a little clarified butter, turn over and similarly cook on the other side. Both sides of the *parantha* should be crisp and delicately browned

5. Remove and serve immediately.

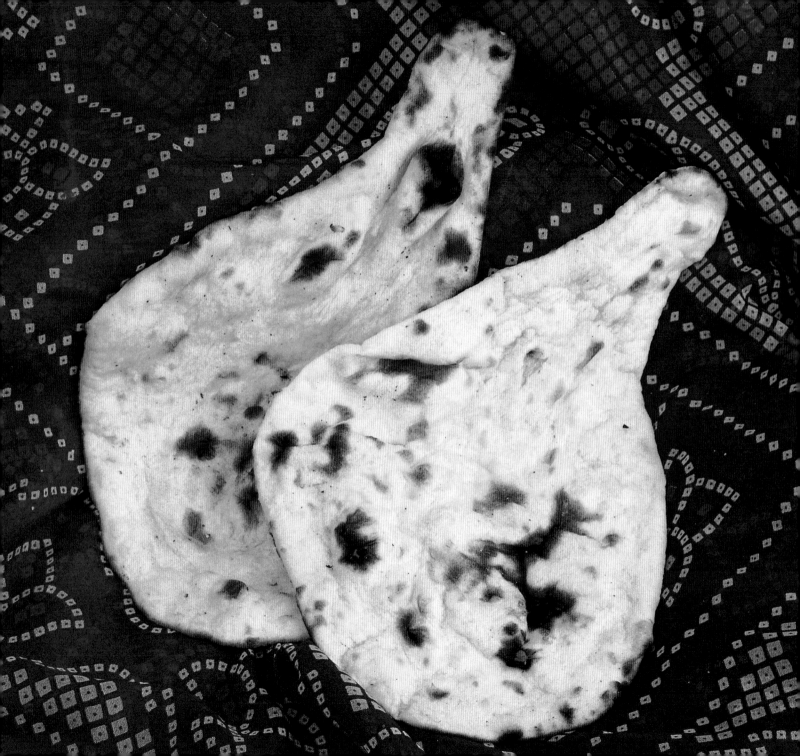

Naan

Serves: 4-5   Preparation time: 3 hours   Cooking time: 20 minutes

Ingredients:

Flour, sieved ....*500 gms / 2½ cups*   Sugar .... *10 gms / 2 tsp*
Salt to taste   Milk .... *50 ml / 3²/₃ tbs*
Baking soda................................. *1 gm / ¼ tsp*   Clarified butter (*ghee*)/Oil ....*25 gms / 5 tsp*
Baking powder............................ *5 gms / 1 tsp*   Onion (*kalonji*) seeds .... *3 gms / ²/₃ tsp*
Egg, whisked ....*1*   Melon (*magaz*) seeds ....*5 gms / 1 tsp*

Method:

1. Mix flour, salt, baking soda, baking powder, egg, sugar and milk. Add enough water to knead into a soft and smooth dough. Cover with a moist cloth, keep aside for 10 minutes.
2. Add oil, knead and punch the dough, cover and keep aside to ferment for 2 hours.
3. Divide the dough into 6 balls, place on a lightly floured surface, sprinkle onion and melon seeds, flatten the balls slightly, cover and keep aside for 5 minutes.
4. Flatten each ball to make a round disc, stretch on one side to form an elongated oval. Place on a greased baking tray. Bake in a preheated oven (175 °C / 350 °F) for 2-3 minutes
5. Serve hot, as an accompaniment to any curry dish.

Chappatis

Serves: 4-6   Preparation time: ½ hour   Cooking time: ½ hour

Ingredients:

Whole wheat flour, sieved ... *225 gms / 2 cups*   Water .... *150 ml / ¾ cup*
Salt (optional) ....*3 gms / ½ tsp*   Clarified butter (*ghee*) .... *15 gms / 1 tbs*

Method:

1. Mix flour and salt in a bowl. Add water, knead into a smooth and elastic dough. Cover and keep aside for 20 minutes at room temperature.
2. Place the dough on a floured board. Divide into 8 portions, roll out each into a thin round, the size of a snack plate.
3. Heat a *tawa* (griddle). Place one round on the griddle. Cook until tiny spots appear on one side, flip over and cook the other side for a few seconds. Flip over again and roast till it is of pale golden colour on both sides.
4. Brush lightly with butter and serve hot, as an accompaniment to any curry dish.

◀ *Naan*

Lamb Biryani

Serves: 4   Preparation time: 30 minutes   Cooking time: 1½ hours

Ingredients:

Lamb (cut into 1" cubes) .... *1 kg*
Basmati rice .... *400 gms / 2 cups*
Oil .... *105 ml / 7 tbs*
Onions, chopped .... *120 gms / ½ cup*
Green cardamoms (*choti elaichi*) *5*
Cloves (*laung*) *2*
Cinnamon (*daalchini*) stick (1") *1*
Yoghurt, whisked .... *120 gms / ½ cup*
Yellow chilli powder .... *5 gms / 1 tsp*
Salt to taste

Lamb stock .... *400 ml / 2 cups*
Mace (*javitri*) powder .... *a pinch*
Mint leaves, chopped .... *5 gms / 1 tsp*
Ginger, chopped .... *30 gms / 2 tbs*
Vetivier (*kewda*) .... *a few drops*
Cream .... *120 ml / ½ cup*
Butter, melted .... *45 gms / 3 tbs*
Saffron (*kesar*) .... *a pinch*
Dough to seal dish
Ginger, julienned .... *5 gms / 1 tsp*

Method:

1. Heat oil in a pan and sauté chopped onions. Add cardamoms, cloves and cinnamon in the oil till they crackle, then add lamb pieces and sauté.

2. Add yoghurt, yellow chilli powder and salt. Stir till dry. Add stock and cook till meat is almost done.

3. In a separate pan, boil rice in plenty of water till the grains lengthen but are not fully cooked. Drain the water.

4. Remove meat pieces from curry and spread in a heat-proof casserole. Strain the curry. Reserve half of the curry and pour the remaining onto the meat. Sprinkle mace, mint, chopped ginger, vetivier and half the cream over the meat.

5. Place half the rice on the meat pieces. Sprinkle reserved cream, the reserved liquid, melted butter and saffron, crushed in a spoonful of water over it.

6. Place rest of the rice on top. Cover and seal lid with dough. Cook over very gentle heat for about 10-15 minutes. Remove from heat, garnish with julienned ginger.

7. Serve hot, accompanied by Mixed Vegetable Raita (page 79).

Note: Substitute lamb with chicken for **Chicken Biryani**.

◀ *Lamb Biryani*

Mixed Vegetable Raita

Serves: 3-4   Preparation time: 15 minutes

Ingredients

Yoghurt .... *600 gm / ¾ cups*
Cumin (*jeera*) seeds .... *5 gm / 1 tsp*
Coriander seeds .... *5 gm / 1 tsp*
Black peppercorns .... *2.5 gm / ½ tsp*
Salt to taste
Cucumber, chopped .... *30 gm / 2 tbs*

Green chilli, finely chopped .... *5 gm / 1 tsp*
Mint, chopped .... *5 gm / 1 tsp*
Onions, chopped .... *30 gm / 3 tbs*
Tomatoes, chopped .... *30 gm / 2 tbs*
Chilli powder to sprinkle .... *a pinch*

Method:

1. Heat a *tawa* (griddle) and broil cumin, coriander seeds and pepper till dark and aromatic.
2. Pound and keep aside.
3. Whisk yoghurt with salt. Add and mix all chopped vegetables.
4. Sprinkle red chilli powder and refrigerate for ½ hour.
5. Serve, as an accompaniment to any curry dish and rice.

Mint Raita

Serves: 4   Preparation time: 10 minutes

Ingredients:

Yoghurt .... *600 ml / 3 cups*
Mint leaves, dried, crushed ...... *75 gms / 5 tbs*

Cumin (*jeera*) powder .... *2.5 gms / ½ tsp*

Method:

1. In a bowl, whisk yoghurt alongwith salt and cumin powder.
2. Add the mint leaves.
3. Refrigerate for half an hour.
4. Sprinkle mint leaves (1 tbs) and serve as an accompaniment to any dish.

◀ *Mixed Vegetable Raita*

Ras Malai

Serves: 8   Preparation time: 1 hour   Cooking time: 1½ hour

Ingredients:

For the flavoured milk:

Whole milk .... *1 litre / 5 cups*
Cream ....*240 ml / 1¹/₃ cup*
Sugar .... *55 gms / 1¹/₃ cup*
Green cardamom (*choti
elaichi*) seeds, crushed .... *5 gms / 1 tsp*

For the filling:

Saffron threads ....*a pinch*
Cream ....*22 ml / 1 ½ tbs*
Pistachios, blanched, minced *15 gms / 1 tbs*

Golden raisens, minced .... *15 gms / 1 tbs*
Almonds, blanched, minced ..... *15 gms / 1tbs*
Honey ....*7 ml / ½ tbs*

For the medallions:

Whole milk ....*2 liters / 10 cups*
Lemon juice, strained ....*60 ml / 4 tbs*
Water ....*1.5 liters/ 7 cups*
Sugar .... *1 kg / 5 cups*
Cornstarch (dissolved) .... *2 tbs*

Method:

1. **For the flavoured milk,** boil milk in a heavy bottomed pan over high heat, till it reduces to a cup, stirring constantly. Add cream, sugar, cardamom, boil for 5 minutes. Pour into a shallow serving dish.
2. **For the filling,** roast the saffron threads and powder with a spoon. Mix with cream, nuts, raisins and honey. Apply a film of oil on hands and divide the filling into 16 portions.
3. **For the medallions,** take milk in a heavy bottomed pan, bring to a frothing boil. Reduce heat. Add lemon juice and stir to make the milk curdle and the cheese to separate from the whey. If the cheese does not separate then add another tbs of lemon juice. Remove from heat and set aside for 10 minutes.
4. Pour cheese mixture into a moist cheese cloth, gather the 4 corners of cloth and rinse under tap water for 10 minutes. Gently twist the cloth to squeeze out excess water. Tie the corners and hang for 20 minutes to allow excess water to drain.
5. Meanwhile, mix water and sugar in a pan, bring to a boil, stirring constantly until the sugar dissolves completely. Cook on high heat for 3-4 minutes, remove from heat and set aside.
6. Unwrap the cheese on a clean work surface, crumble it repeatedly till it becomes fluffy and smooth. Collect all the cheese into one big portion and divide into 16 portions. Place one portion of filling in each portion of cheese and shape each into a medallion.
7. Reheat the sugar syrup, bring to a boil and slide in the prepared medallions. Increase heat and boil continuously for about 20 minutes adding cornstarch with ¼ cup water after 4

◀ *Ras Malai*

minutes of boiling. Thereafter, ¼ cup of water after every 4 minutes to maintain the consistency of syrup. Take care to add the water directly into the syrup and not on the medallions. Remove from heat and cool.

8. Gently lift the medallions with a slotted spoon, drain and slip them into the flavoured milk, garnish with vetivier essence, refrigerate for upto 6 hours.
9. Serve chilled in small dishes with a few tablespoon of flavoured milk.

Kesar Sandesh

Serves: 4   Preparation time: 1½ hour   Cooking time: 1 hour

Ingredients:

Saffron (*kesar*) ....*3 gms / ½ tsp*   Lemon juice ....*60 ml / ½ tbs*
Whole milk ....*320 ml / 1½ cups*   Sugar, powdered ....*110 gms / ½ cups*

Method:

1. Roast saffron in a dry pan and pound to a fine powder. Dissolve in hot milk (2 tbs) and keep aside.
2. Heat milk in a pan over high heat, bring to a frothing boil, stirring continuously. Reduce heat, add lemon juice to make the milk curdle and the cheese to separate from the whey. If it does not, then add another tbs of lemon juice. Remove from heat and set aside to cool.
3. Pour the cheese-whey mixture into a moist cheese cloth, gather the 4 corners of the cloth and rinse under tap water for 10 minutes. Gently twist the cloth to squeeze out excess water. Tie up the corners and hang for 20-30 minutes to allow all excess water to drain.
4. Unwrap the cheese on a clean work surface and crumble repeatedly till it becomes fluffy and even. Blend in the powdered sugar and knead till it becomes smooth and grainless.
5. Transfer cheese-sugar (*chenna*) mixture to a heavy bottomed pan, cook for 10-15 minutes until mixture becomes a little thickened and glossy.
6. Divide the mixture into two portions. Mix in the dissolved saffron into one portion till it is thoroughly mixed and turns yellow. Divide the yellow *chenna* mixture into 2 portions again.
7. Spread three alternate layers of yellow, white and yellow *chenna* on a buttered tray to form a 1½"-2" thick cake. Allow to cool and cut into 1½" thick squares and serve at room temperature or slightly cooled.

◀ *Kesar Sandesh*

INDEX